GROUND
BREAKERS
BLACK
MUSICIANS

LIZZO

by Joyce Markovics

Cherry Lake Press
Ann Arbor, Michigan

Cherry Lake Press

Published in the United States of America by Cherry Lake Publishing
Ann Arbor, Michigan
www.cherrylakepublishing.com

Reading Adviser: Beth Walker Gambro, MS, Ed., Reading Consultant, Yorkville, IL
Content Adviser: Michael Kramer, PhD, Music Historian
Book Designer: Ed Morgan

Photo Credits: © Doug Peters/Alamy Stock Photo, cover and title page; © Paul R Giunta/Invision/AP/Shutterstock, 5; freepik.com, 6; Wikimedia Commons/Lennon Photography, 7; freepik.com, 8; © Paul Froggatt/Alamy Stock Photo, 9; © Media Punch Inc/Alamy Stock Photo, 11; Wikimedia Commons, 12; © Paul Froggatt/Alamy Stock Photo, 13; © JEP Live Music/Alamy Stock Photo, 14; © ZUMA Press, Inc./Alamy Stock Photo, 15; © Matt Sayles/Invision/AP/Shutterstock, 16; © Ben Houdijk/Shutterstock, 17; © Doug Peters/Alamy Stock Photo, 18; © LOC Photo/Alamy Stock Photo, 19; © Image Press Agency/NurPhoto/Shutterstock, 21; freepik.com, 22.

Copyright © 2024 by Cherry Lake Publishing Group

All rights reserved. No part of this book may be reproduced or utilized in any form or by any means without written permission from the publisher.

Cherry Lake Press is an imprint of Cherry Lake Publishing Group.

Library of Congress Cataloging-in-Publication Data

Names: Markovics, Joyce L., author.
Title: Lizzo / by Joyce Markovics.
Description: Ann Arbor, Michigan : Cherry Lake Publishing, 2023. | Series: Groundbreakers: Black musicians | Includes bibliographical references and index. | Audience: Grades 4-6
Identifiers: LCCN 2023003476 (print) | LCCN 2023003477 (ebook) | ISBN 9781668927847 (hardcover) | ISBN 9781668928899 (paperback) | ISBN 9781668930366 (epub) | ISBN 9781668931844 (pdf) | ISBN 9781668933329 (kindle edition) | ISBN 9781668934807 (ebook)
Subjects: LCSH: Lizzo, 1988—Juvenile literature. | Singers—United States—Biography—Juvenile literature. | Rap musicians—United States—Biography—Juvenile literature. | Flute players—United States—Biography—Juvenile literature.
Classification: LCC ML3930.L579 M27 2023 (print) | LCC ML3930.L579 (ebook) | DDC 782.42164092 [B]—dc23/eng/20230125
LC record available at https://lccn.loc.gov/2023003476
LC ebook record available at https://lccn.loc.gov/2023003477

Printed in the United States of America by
Corporate Graphics

Note from publisher: Websites change regularly, and their future contents are outside of our control. Supervise children when conducting any recommended online searches for extended learning opportunities.

CONTENTS

This Is Lizzo............ 4
Early Life 6
Making Music 12
Lizzo's Impact.......... 20

Greatest Hits................22
Glossary....................23
Find Out More 24
Index......................24
About the Author............24

THIS IS LIZZO

Lizzo is more than a global superstar. This talented singer, rapper, and **flutist** spreads joy with her music. Through her playful and powerful lyrics, Lizzo talks about her struggles and **triumphs**. She encourages her fans to accept and love themselves—no matter their size, skin color, or **gender**. Lizzo has earned countless awards, including several Grammys. And this groundbreaker's star is still rising.

> "I HAVE TO FIND THE SOUL IN EVERYTHING."
> —LIZZO

Melissa Viviane Jefferson, also known as Lizzo

One of Lizzo's **mantras** is, "You are beautiful. And you can do anything."

5

EARLY LIFE

On April 27, 1988, Melissa "Lizzo" Viviane Jefferson was born in the city of Detroit, Michigan. She was the youngest of three siblings. Lizzo's parents worked hard running several businesses. But they always made time for family. And they pushed their children to do their best. "My mother and father taught me about Black excellence," said Lizzo.

Lizzo's hometown of Detroit, Michigan

As a kid, Lizzo dreamed of being a writer or a scientist. "I spent a lot of time star-gazing, writing, and learning languages," said Lizzo. She also loved music, which filled her home. "I was raised on **gospel**," she said. Thanks to her dad, Lizzo also listened to pop and rock music, including Elton John and Queen.

Lizzo in her youth

Lizzo was sometimes teased "for wanting to be intelligent, for reading, for talking the way I do," she said. "But I didn't dumb myself down just to be accepted."

7

When Lizzo was 9 years old, her family moved to Houston, Texas. It was a **culture shock**. Her new home was surrounded by farms and fields. "There were kids who used to ride their horses to school," Lizzo remembers. She felt out of place. Then in sixth grade, Lizzo's music teacher asked if she wanted to play the flute. Lizzo happily agreed. "I started to listen to music and obsess over music," she said.

> "NEVER EVER LET SOMEONE STOP YOU OR SHAME YOU FROM BEING YOURSELF."
> —LIZZO

Lizzo's classmates said she smiled too much and laughed too loud. They made fun of her clothes. Music was an escape for Lizzo. Every day, Lizzo practiced her flute. She proudly played in the band. "I wanted to be the best flute player ever," Lizzo said.

Melissa got the nickname Lizzo in middle school. Here she is playing the flute as an adult.

Lizzo enjoyed **anime** and reading comic books when she was young. She especially liked the comic *Sailor Moon*.

As a teen, Lizzo also loved rapping and dancing. Even then, she was a natural performer. At 14, Lizzo formed a rap group, the Cornrow Clique, with her friends. To practice her skills, she **freestyled** on the bus, at school, and anywhere else she could. That same year, Lizzo joined the marching band. "I was the baddest **piccolo** player in the land," she said. But the teasing got worse. Lizzo was targeted for being big, weird, and Black. Lizzo described her young self as a "dorky, overweight teen." She didn't fit in with the other kids. And she felt bad about her body.

> "I AM MY INSPIRATION."
> —LIZZO

When Lizzo got her license as a teenager, she was afraid to drive. "The police were right behind you," she said. Even though Lizzo **obeyed** every traffic law, she got pulled over many times. This is a common experience for Black drivers. People of other races are much less likely to be pulled over for no reason.

Lizzo has enjoyed dancing since she was a kid.

MAKING MUSIC

In spite of her daily struggles, Lizzo focused on the flute. She dreamed of playing in a **symphony** one day. When Lizzo earned a music **scholarship** to attend the University of Houston, she was **ecstatic**. She majored in classical flute performance. She joined her college's marching band. But by her junior year, Lizzo felt trapped and overwhelmed. She made the hard decision to drop out of college.

The University of Houston

"I DON'T THINK THAT LOVING YOURSELF IS A CHOICE. I THINK THAT IT'S A DECISION THAT HAS TO BE MADE FOR SURVIVAL."
—LIZZO

By that time, Lizzo's parents had left Texas. To get by, Lizzo slept in her car and on her friends' couches. In 2008, she joined a band called Ellypseas. Her bandmates shared their homes with Lizzo. And she accepted meals from them. Then a family **tragedy** upended Lizzo's already shaky world.

Even at her lowest point, Lizzo continued to make music.

Lizzo struggled to take care of herself after dropping out of college. When there were no other options, Lizzo ate meat even though she is a vegetarian.

In 2009, Lizzo's father died. She sank into a deep **depression**. "My father passed away, I was homeless, I didn't have any money, my band was doing really bad, and I was by myself," remembers Lizzo. She doubted everything, including the way she looked.

Lizzo on stage early in her career

Rapper Missy Elliot is a huge influence on Lizzo's music. "She's so unique, so incredible, so special, so magical," said Lizzo.

After a lot of **self-reflection**, Lizzo picked herself up. "You're not going to wake up and be bigger or smaller or lighter or darker. . . . You're going to look this way for the rest of your life," Lizzo said to herself. "And you have to be OK with that. I used my music as therapy to get there." A year later, Lizzo moved to Minneapolis, Minnesota, to explore the city's music scene. She formed two bands and started getting noticed.

While living in Minneapolis, Lizzo called one of her early bands Lizzo & the Larva Ink.

"MINNEAPOLIS JUST EMBRACED ME. THERE ARE A LOT OF WEIRDOS THERE. IT'S AWESOME, BECAUSE I'M A WEIRDO."
—LIZZO

In Minneapolis, Lizzo started performing solo. In 2013, she released her first album, *Lizzobangers*. **Critics** praised its **originality**. Two years later, she made another album, *Big GRRRL Small World*. A critic raved about her "ability to rap and sing with equal **tenacity**." The album led to a record deal and Lizzo moving to Los Angeles, California. Soon after, Lizzo released *Coconut Oil*. The album was another success. Lizzo became an outspoken supporter of body acceptance. "We should love ourselves first. We should look at our bodies as vehicles for success," said Lizzo.

Lizzo playing her flute, which she named Sasha Flute, after a Beyoncé album.

Lizzo continued to work on her music and herself. In 2019, she dropped a single called "Juice." Her album, *Cuz I Love You*, followed. It climbed the charts. Other hit songs followed, including "Truth Hurts." Lizzo performed "Truth Hurts" and a flute solo at the **BET** Awards. The crowd went wild.

> "TO TRULY BE IN LOVE WITH YOURSELF IS FREEDOM."
> —LIZZO

Lizzo performing in 2019

Lizzo takes the stage with her backup dancers.

Lizzo went on tour to **promote** her album. She performed many sold-out shows. Then she opened the 62nd Annual Grammy Awards and won three awards! Her career was skyrocketing. In 2020, Lizzo began work on a new album. The album, *Special*, came out in 2022 to rave reviews.

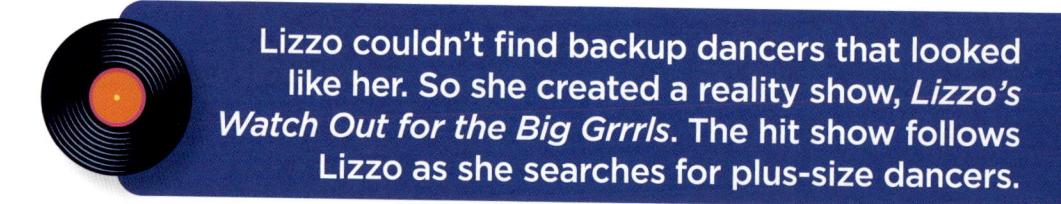

Lizzo couldn't find backup dancers that looked like her. So she created a reality show, *Lizzo's Watch Out for the Big Grrrls*. The hit show follows Lizzo as she searches for plus-size dancers.

That same year, Lizzo was invited to play a glass flute from 1813 that once belonged to President James Madison! Lizzo was floored. "It's crystal, it's like playing out of a wine glass," she said. Lizzo played a few notes on the priceless flute for her fans. "We just made history tonight!" she said.

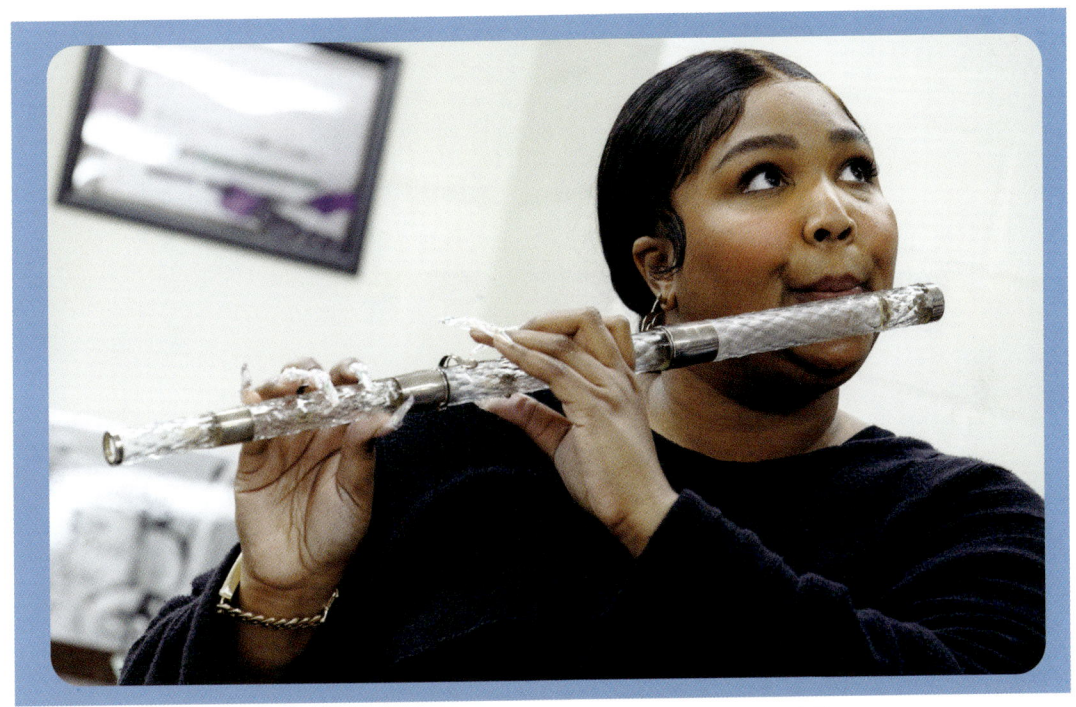

Lizzo plays President James Madison's crystal flute

"AS A FAT BLACK WOMAN IN AMERICA, I'VE HAD MANY HURTFUL WORDS USED AGAINST ME SO I 'OVERSTAND' THE POWER WORDS CAN HAVE."
—LIZZO

LIZZO'S IMPACT

Later in 2022, Lizzo was honored with a People's Champion Award. In her speech, Lizzo paid tribute to 17 other **activists**. "Ever since the beginning of my career, I used my platform to **amplify marginalized voices**," said Lizzo. "Tonight, I'm sharing that honor."

Lizzo has never forgotten where she came from. She inspires people to accept themselves for who they are. "Every time I rap about being a big girl in a small world, it's doing a couple things: it's **empowering** my self-awareness, my body image, and it's also making the statement . . . we're a part of something bigger than this," said Lizzo. She truly is a people's champion.

> "BEING AN ICON IS WHAT YOU *DO* WITH THAT PLATFORM."
> —LIZZO

"I work on myself daily to be a better person," said Lizzo.

For years, Lizzo has been bullied and received hate comments for being a plus-size Black woman. "I've been broken-hearted by this country," said Lizzo. However, Lizzo believes in standing up and speaking out.

GREATEST HITS

Here's are some of Lizzo's signature songs:

Truth Hurts

My Skin

Juice

Worship

Boys

Tempo

Jerome

Rumors

Cuz I Love You

2 Be Loved (Am I Ready)

✳ Some of these songs include words that might not be appropriate for young people. Please talk to a parent or an adult before listening.

GLOSSARY

activists (AK-tuh-vists) people who fight for a cause

amplify (AM-pluh-fye) to increase in strength or sound

anime (AN-uh-mey) a style of Japanese film and animation

BET (BEE-EE-TEE) stands for Black Entertainment Television

critics (KRIT-iks) people who judge something

culture shock (KUHL-cher SHOK) a state of confusion by a person in a new environment

depression (di-PRESH-uhn) a medical condition in which a person can feel sad, tired, and hopeless

ecstatic (ek-STAT-ik) related to sudden, intense emotion

empowering (em-POW-er-ing) making something more powerful

flutist (FLOO-tist) a flute player

freestyled (FREE-stiled) made up something, such as a rap or song

gender (JEN-dur) identities that relate to being female or male

gospel (GOS-puhl) a style of religious music

mantras (MAN-truhs) repeated words or phrases

marginalized voices (MAHR-juh-nul-ahyzd VOIS-uhz) the voices of people who have little power or influence

obeyed (oh-BAYD) followed orders

originality (uh-rij-uh-NAL-ih-tee) the quality of being special and interesting

piccolo (PIK-uh-loh) a small flute

promote (pruh-MOHT) to build the popularity of something

scholarship (SKOL-ur-ship) an award that helps pay for a person to go to college

self-reflection (SELF ri-FLEKT-shun) serious thought about who a person is and their actions

symphony (SIM-fuh-nee) a large orchestra made up of different instruments

tenacity (tuh-NAS-ih-tee) the state of holding onto something

tragedy (TRAJ-uh-dee) a sad and terrible event

triumphs (TRAHY-uhmfs) great victories

23

FIND OUT MORE

BOOKS

Levy, Joel. *Turn It Up! A Pitch-Perfect History of Music That Rocked the World*. Washington, DC: National Geographic Kids, 2019.

Richards, Mary, and David Schweitzer. *A History of Music for Children*. London, UK: Thames & Hudson, 2021.

Wilson, Lakita. *Lizzo: Breakout Artist*. Minneapolis, MN: Lerner, 2021.

WEBSITES
Explore these online sources with an adult:

Grammy Awards: Lizzo

Learning for Justice: Lizzo

Lizzo Official Website

INDEX

albums, 16–18
backup dancers, 18
BET Awards, 17
body acceptance, 15–16, 20
Cornrow Clique, 10
Ellypseas, 13
Grammy Awards, 4, 18
hit songs, 17, 22
homelessness, 13–14
Lizzo
   bullying, 10, 21
   childhood, 7–9
   early influences, 7

family, 6, 8, 13–14
flute, 8–9, 12, 19
impact, 20
marching band, 10, 12
name, 6
Madison flute, 19
Minneapolis, 15–16
racism, 11
rap, 4, 10, 14, 16, 20
reality show, 18
Texas, 8, 13
touring, 18
University of Houston, 12

ABOUT THE AUTHOR

Joyce Markovics has written hundreds of books for kids. She appreciates the power of music to move and unite us. Joyce is grateful to all people who have beaten the odds to tell their stories and make great art. She encourages her young readers to love themselves and always be kind to others.